Hard At Work

by Laurel Dickey

Pioneer Valley Educational Press, Inc.

Mom is in the kitchen.

Dad is in the kitchen.

Dad is in the living room.

Mom is in the living room.

Dad is in the bathroom.

Mom is in the bathroom.

Mom is outside.

Dad is outside.

Dad is in the bedroom.

Mom is in the bedroom.

Mom is in the garage.

Dad is in the garage.

Mom is in the living room.

Dad is in the living room.